Speak Street was founded as a positive response to negativity towards newcomers. We are a not for profit organisation and offer free ESOL classes, and create workbooks to help ESOL learners through fun, social learning.

To check out more about us, visit
www.speak-street.com

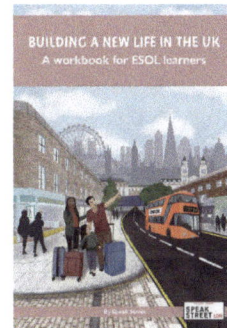

Created by Joanna Bevan
Illustration by Jade Paniganiban & Carl Sullivan

Kindly Supported by Linklaters for Duke's Aldridge Academy

CONTENTS

A [ ]

B [ ]

C [ ]

D [ ]

E [ ]

F [ ]

**Match the words
to the pictures**

1. **Nursery / Pre-school**
2. **Primary school**
3. **Secondary school**
4. **College**
5. **Private school**
6. **Selective school**
7. **Ofsted**
8. **SEND (Special Educational
   Needs & Disabilities)
   School**
9. **Home school**

G [ ]

H [ ]

I [ ]

Reading

Maryam has just moved to Tottenham, London with her family.
She meets her new neighbour, Danisha for the first time.

Hello, do you need help? That box looks heavy.	Welcome to Tottenham, wow your English is really good for a **newcomer**!	Great, how old are your kids? I have two daughters and a son myself. Maya is fifteen, Ray is nine and Viva is four.
I'm ok thanks, this is the last box. We moved in yesterday with my children. I'm Maryam. We're new to the UK.	I studied English at school and I watch a lot of English films.	Elena is fourteen and Alex is eight . I need to look for schools for them, but I'm unsure how it works here.
Alex would go to **primary school** until he's eleven. Viva will start in September. I'm just on my way to pick her up from nursery.	Ray needs a bit of extra help as he has some health conditions, so he goes to a **special educational needs school**.	Yeah, my whole life. I know all the schools around here. When you've unpacked, why don't you come round for tea one day and we can chat about it?
Thanks, which school does your son go to?	Have you lived here a long time?	Thank you, that would be lovely.

Can you create your own sentences with each highlighted word/phrase?

Writing

In the UK, boys and girls start school at age 5, and stay in education until they are 18. What would you like to study ?

_____

_____

_____

CHAPTER 2 - CHOOSING A SCHOOL

(A) _____

(B) _____

(C) _____

(D) _____

(E) _____

(F) _____

(G) _____

(H) _____

(I) _____

Match the words to the pictures

1. **Breakfast club**
2. **After school club**
3. **Outdoor learning**
4. **Awards**
5. **Results**
6. **Diversity**
7. **Religious values**
8. **School equipment**
9. **Parent communication**
10. **School leadership**
11. **School application form**

(J) _____

(K) _____

Reading

Maryam is having coffee with Danisha at her house.

Panel 1:
Do you take milk and sugar in your tea?

Just sugar please, it still seems strange to put milk in tea for me.

Panel 2:
There you go. So, when you're choosing a school, you should visit all the schools with your child and write a list of things you would like. Some people just look at the **Ofsted** report or the exam results, but you should think about other things as well.

Like how far away it is?

Panel 3:
Yes, you have to live in the school's **catchment area**. I think about the ethos of the school and what **facilities** they have - my daughter's school has a swimming pool. Also, she has a severe nut allergy and the school is really good at making sure it has a nut-free environment. For some parents, it's important the school is based on religious values; others want an after school club.

Ok, so it's a bit more complicated than I thought.

Panel 4:
My advice is to go to the community centre on the corner, and talk to other families. They have a great **after school club**. My kids love going there because we don't have a garden and it gives me the chance to go to work. I'd definitely go and visit the schools and make up your own mind.

Can you create your own sentences with each highlighted word/phrase?

Writing

What would you consider when choosing a school?

_____

_____

_____

_____

Vocabulary

A [ ]

B [ ]

C

D [ ]

E [ ]

F [ ]

G [ ]

H [ ]

Match the words to the pictures

1. **Headteacher**
2. **Form teacher / tutor**
3. **Teaching assistant**
4. **Receptionist**
5. **Librarian**
6. **Maintenance staff**
7. **Catering staff**
8. **D&T technician**
9. **Lollipop person**
10. **School counsellor**

I [ ]

J [ ]

CHAPTER 3 - ROLES IN SCHOOL

Maryam is visiting a secondary school open day, with her daughter, Elena. Karim, one of the year eleven students, is showing them around.

That's Mr Yildiz, he is head of the **pastoral team**. They focus on the physical and emotional care of the students. Our school is very **diverse**, we have loads of students with English as a second language, from different religions and backgrounds.

What kind of things does the pastoral team help with?

If students need help with something outside of school work, or if something is stopping students from learning, we have a school counsellor that can help students with problems and worries too. My parents didn't know that teenagers get free bus travel, or I could get free school meals until Mr Yildiz told them. We also have an **anti-bullying** programme.

So there are many more people than just teachers working in the school?

Yes, teaching assistants, facilities team, catering staff. Our school **specialises** in arts and drama. Let me show you the music studio.

I like making music on my laptop, but I always wanted to learn an instrument. My Dad used to play the guitar.

Some of our students go on to become musicians and we have an amazing music teacher here, Mr Randolf. He used to play in a **band**.

Can you create your own sentences with each highlighted word/phrase?

Writing

Who are some of the people you will find working in a school, and what do they do?

_____

_____

_____

_____

Vocabulary

(A)

(B)

(C)

(D)

(E)

(F)

Match the words to the pictures

1. **Tie**
2. **Blazer**
3. **P.E. kit**
4. **Polo shirt**
5. **Skirt**
6. **Summer uniform dress**
7. **Knee socks**
8. **Book bag**
9. **Lunch box**
10. **Rucksack**

(G)

(H)

(I)

(J)

CHAPTER 4 - SCHOOL UNIFORM

Reading

It's August and Danisha spots Maryam on her way to the supermarket.

> Hi Danisha, how are you doing? I'm just going to buy some school uniforms.

> That time of year again! Did you know there is a **second-hand** school uniform shop run by the school? It can really add up when you buy the whole uniform **brand new**.

> Thanks, I didn't know that, that sounds really good. For secondary school, Elena needs a **blazer** and jumper with the school badge on it, and a tie. I need to find some white shirts, black trousers and then there are school shoes of course.

> They have a **special offer** on shirts in the supermarket. My kids hated wearing school uniforms, especially on hot days, but when they had a non-uniform day for World Book Day, it took them so long to decide what to wear. Funnily enough, they were glad when they changed back into their uniforms. There's a great charity shop on the high street. I buy a lot of coats and bags from there. I've got a spare coat that's too small for Ray, it might fit Alex if you like?

> Thanks, I'm so glad I **bumped into** you. It can be so expensive, and they grow up so fast!

Can you create your own sentences with each highlighted word/phrase?

Writing

Do you think it's better to have a school uniform or wear your own clothes to school?

_____

_____

_____

_____

Vocabulary

(A)

_____

(B)

_____

(C)

_____

(D)

_____

(E)

_____

(F)

_____

Match the words to the pictures

1. **Mobile phone**
2. **Bullying**
3. **Detention**
4. **No knives**
5. **No drugs**
6. **Lateness**
7. **Attendance**
8. **Truancy**
9. **Homework**

(G)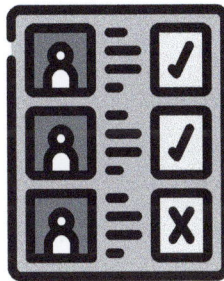

_____

(H)

_____

(I)

_____

CHAPTER 5 - SCHOOL RULES

Reading

Elena and her Mum are registering for her new school. Mrs Taylor, the receptionist is helping her.

You have to sign this form.

What is it?

It's the parent **agreement**. Parents have to agree to the school rules. It says students are not allowed to use their mobile phones in school, they have to **respect** everyone, they mustn't be late and can get detention if they break any of the rules.

What's **detention**?

If they break the rules, the student has to stay indoors and do extra work at break time, or even after school.

That sounds fair enough, but I know Elena will behave and probably never get detention. Here's the signed form.

Thank you, so next we need to set up Parent Pay.

It's so students can pay for lunch **electronically**, and not have to carry cash to school.

What's that?

Can you create your own sentences with each highlighted word?

Writing

Do you think students should be allowed to use mobile phones in school?

_____

_____

_____

_____

Vocabulary

(A)

(B)

(C)

(D)

(E)

(F)

Match the words to the pictures

1. **English**
2. **Maths**
3. **Science**
4. **History**
5. **Geography**
6. **French**
7. **Art**
8. **Music**
9. **Food technology**
10. **P.E.**

(G)

(H)

(I)

(J)

CHAPTER 6 - SCHOOL SUBJECTS

Reading

Elena is thinking about her GCSE options. She asks her neighbour Maya, for some advice.

Hi Elena, how's your new school going?

Yeah I like it, we have to think about which GCSEs we want to choose next year. Do you have any **advice**?

I'm revising for mine right now. I think I would say firstly choose the subjects you love.

I love French, history and art, but I was thinking I'm not sure if that will help me in the future. I'm a bit worried about English. I find spelling so difficult.

Do you have an idea of what you want to do in the future, because I don't? Some people just follow their friends, but I think the most important thing is to choose the subject that's best for you. I speak Spanish with my Dad and I found out I could do an extra Spanish **GCSE**, so maybe you can do a GSCE in your own language too?

That's a good idea.

If you are not sure about the subject, you can also ask the teachers and look at the **syllabus**.

What's the syllabus?

It's information about all the things you will learn on the course. OK, I'd better get back to revising, I have a **mock exam** tomorrow.

OK thanks Maya, good luck!

Can you create your own sentences with each highlighted word/phrase?

Writing

Which subjects are you interested in? How can you find out more about different subjects?

Vocabulary

s	a	t	p	i	n	m	d
g	o	c	k	_ck	e	u	r
h	b	f	_ff	l	_ll	_ss	j
v	w	_x	y	z	_ zz	qu	ch
sh	th	_ng	ai	ee	igh	oa	oo
oo	ar	or	ur	ow	oi	ear	air
ure	er						

Try sounding out the words yourself. Use the pictures to help you determine the sound.

CHAPTER 7 - PHONICS

Reading

Danisha is attending a phonics session at primary school, run by Mr Abedi.

What is **phonics** exactly?

It's a technique for teaching children how to read and write. We teach the sounds of each letter of the alphabet, and then the sounds of groups of letters. Take the word 'cat,' for example. We start by sounding out the first letter, then the next, then the last; c-a-t. We then **blend** them all together, 'cat'.

I don't remember learning this at school.

It's how we teach children to read nowadays. It's a **logical** system. You can help them a lot at home by reading out the sounds with them. It can also help adults learn to read and spell.

I see, so it's building up the words as you read them, bit by bit.

Exactly!

Can you create your own sentences with each highlighted word?

Writing

Write down any tips you know to learn spellings.

_____

_____

_____

_____

14

Vocabulary

A

_____

B _____

C _____

D

_____

E _____

Match the words to the pictures

1. Improvement
2. Achievement
3. Grades
4. Questions
5. Feedback
6. Appointment
7. Discussion

F _____

G _____

CHAPTER 8 - PARENTS' EVENING

Reading

Elena's Mum is speaking to Mrs Timor at Parents' Evening.

Hello, I'm Elena's Mum.

Hello, I'm Elena's class tutor. She's been doing very well. She's **hardworking**. Though, one thing she needs to improve on is her literacy.

Yes, she's still learning English, I think she finds spelling hard, and she says she doesn't want to read aloud in class.

Children her age catch up very quickly. I've recommended her for a special programme here in school, to help improve her reading and writing.

I feel bad because I can't help her much.

Why don't you sign up for the library? She'll improve a lot faster if she reads more in English, and it's free! Sometimes it helps to watch TV with the **subtitles** on too.

OK yes, good idea. Do you think she gets on well with the other students? She is very **shy**, and I'm worried she hasn't made any friends yet.

She seems to have a few friends she sits next to. When students are new, we pair them up with a buddy to help them settle in.

That's good to hear. It's been good speaking with you. Next, I have to meet with her Maths tutor.

Can you create your own sentences with each highlighted word/phrase?

Writing

What questions would you ask a teacher at parents' evening?

_____

_____

_____

Vocabulary

(A)

(B)

(C)

(D)

(E)

(F)

(G)

(H)

Match the words to the pictures

1. **Coach**
2. **Bus pass**
3. **Permission slip**
4. **Museum**
5. **Stadium**
6. **Art gallery**
7. **Activity centre**
8. **Packed lunch**
9. **Trip abroad**
10. **Theatre**

(I)

(J)

Reading

Maya's class is going on a field trip to a law firm.

Hi, I'm Ronan, welcome to Linklaters. We are one of the largest law firms in the country. Can anyone guess how many people work here?

One hundred and fifty?

Not even close. It's over five thousand. We have different types of employees, including lawyers, **paralegals**, caterers, security staff, even fitness instructors. Now, let's see if we can think about what skills are needed for each job. Then we'll have a tour and meet some of them.

I think for a lawyer, you need to have good attention to detail. You need to be hard-working and have good presentation skills.

Excellent, can you tell me what skills you have, and what you would like to improve on?

I like public speaking and working in a team, but I could be better at **numeracy**.

That's one of the great things about working in a team, everyone can share their knowledge and skills, and help each other to improve.

Can you create your own sentences with each highlighted word?

Writing

Do you think school trips are important? What kind of days out would you enjoy?

_____

_____

_____

_____

Vocabulary

A [   ]

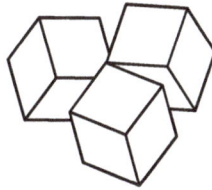

B [   ]

C [   ]

D [   ]

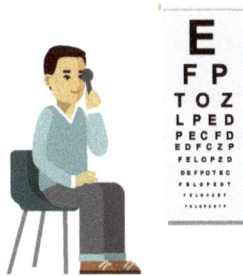

E [   ]

F [   ]

Match the words to the pictures

1. **Mental health**
2. **Sugar levels**
3. **Dental hygiene**
4. **Fitness**
5. **Healthy relationships**
6. **Fibre**
7. **Meditation**
8. **Eyesight**
9. **Drinking water**
10. **Therapy**

G [   ]

H [   ]

I [   ]

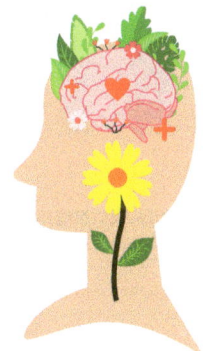

J [   ]

Reading

Danisha is helping Maya with her homework.

Panel 1: Mum, I've got to give a presentation on "Healthy Habits" tomorrow. Can you help me practise? What do you have so far?

Panel 2: Here are five healthy habits. Number 1: eat a **balanced diet**, with at least five fruits and vegetables a day. An easy way to eat them is in a smoothie for breakfast, or have them in a packed lunch. Number 2: drink six to eight cups of water a day to stay hydrated. Eating and drinking well will help you stay healthy and able to concentrate.

Panel 3: Is that right? Hang on, I need to get some more water now. Healthy habit number 3: stay positive and aim high. This will help you stay resilient when you face any problem. Number 4: think of things you are **grateful** for every day.

Panel 4: I am grateful for your advice!

Panel 5: Number 5: make sure you do a little bit of exercise every day. Even walking is good if you don't like playing sports. Finally, number 6: make sure you get a good night's sleep; try to get eight hours and you'll feel fresh and ready to start the day.

Panel 6: Very good presentation! What about including something like, limiting **screen time**? It's getting late so you better follow your own advice and go to bed.

Can you create your own sentences with each highlighted word/phrase?

Writing

What are some of the ways to stay healthy?

_____

_____

_____

_____

Vocabulary

A _____

B _____

C _____

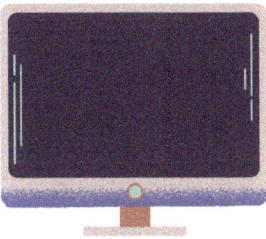

D _____

E _____

F _____

G _____

H _____

I _____

J _____

Match the words to the pictures

1. **Mouse**
2. **Tablet**
3. **Charger**
4. **Video game**
5. **Screen**
6. **Keyboard**
7. **Scam**
8. **Parental locks**
9. **Social media**
10. **Cyber bullying**

CHAPTER 11 - ONLINE SAFETY

Reading

Maryam gets an email from school about parent e-safety. It gives parents tips to help their child stay safe online.

From: office@tworiversacademy.sch.org

Re: Staying safe online

Dear Parent/Guardian,

Here are some tips to help your child stay safe online:

- Talk to your child about their online life. Young people use the internet to **socialise**, do school work, pass the time and more. If your child knows you understand their usage on the internet, they are more likely to ask you if they need help.
- Keep up to date with the technology your child uses online.
- Set **boundaries** in the online world, just like you do in the real world. Think about what they might see, what they share, who they talk to and how long they spend online.
- Know which devices you have connected to the internet and how.
- Consider the use of **parental controls** on devices that link to the internet. Parental controls help you to set appropriate boundaries.
- Emphasise that not everyone is who they say they are. Make sure your child understands that they should never meet up with anyone they only know online, without taking a trusted adult with them.
- Know what to do if something goes wrong. Just like in the real world, you want to be able to help your child when they need it.

Send   A   0 ⊂⊃   🗑 ▾

Can you create your own sentences with each highlighted word/phrase?

Writing

How can children stay safe online?

_____

_____

_____

_____

Vocabulary

(A)

(B)

(C)

(D)

(E)

(F)

(G)

Match the words to the pictures

1. **Apprenticeship**
2. **Entrepreneur**
3. **University degree**
4. **T. Levels**
5. **C.V.**
6. **Careers advisor**
7. **Vocational training**
8. **Mentor**

(H)

Reading

Maya is visiting a college open day with her friend, Sami.

Sami: Where shall we start? There are lots of talks and **demonstrations** we can go to.	**Sami:** OK, after that I want to check and see if there's anything connected to the police. I was thinking about joining the police force. I love crime dramas. I think I'd be a great detective.
Maya: Let's watch the cookery demonstration, I was thinking about becoming a chef. Oh look, Ryan's over there running on a **treadmill**. That must be the sports science section.	**Maya:** So, did you change your mind about applying to University?
Maya: No, I just want to keep my options open. I'm also working on my own business idea; **drop shipping** phone accessories.	**Sami:** Yes, that's true. Oh look, there's going to be a Q&A Let's check out the talk about becoming a police officer.
Sami: Why not do both? It's always good to have a **side hustle**!	**Maya:** OK, great, but after the cookery demonstration. Hopefully, we can try the food. I'm sooo hungry!

Can you create your own sentences with each highlighted word/phrase?

Writing

When young people reach the age of 18, they can apply for university, or get a job – what would you choose and why?

_____

_____

_____

ANSWERS

Ch. 1 - BRITISH SCHOOL SYSTEM
p1
1-A 2-D 3-C 4-I 5-B 6-H 7-F 8-G
9-E

Ch. 2 - CHOOSING A SCHOOL
p3
1-A 2-D 3-B 4-C 5-I 6-E 7-J 8-K
9-H 10-G 11-F

Ch. 3 - ROLES IN SCHOOL
p5
1-D 2-I 3-B 4-J 5-F 6-G 7-E 8-C
9-H 10-A

Ch. 4 - SCHOOL UNIFORM
p7
1-A 2-E 3-B 4-I 5-D 6-F 7-G 8-H
9-C 10-J

Ch. 5 - SCHOOL RULES
p9
1-C 2-B 3-I 4-E 5-A 6-D 7-G 8-H
9-F

Ch. 6 - SCHOOL SUBJECTS
p11
1-I 2-E 3-A 4-B 5-G 6-H 7-C 8-J
9-D 10-F

Ch. 8 - PARENTS' EVENING
p15
1-D 2-B 3-F 4-A 5-G 6-C 7-E

Ch. 9 - SCHOOL TRIPS
p17
1-A 2-B 3-F 4-D 5-E 6-J 7-C 8-H
9-I 10-G

Ch. 10 - HEALTH AND WELL-BEING
p19
1-J 2-B 3-C 4-D 5-H 6-G 7-I 8-E
9-F 10-A

Ch. 11 - ONLINE SAFETY
p21
1-A 2-B 3-F 4-E 5-D 6-J 7-I 8-H
9-G 10-C

Ch. 12 - POST EXAMS
p23
1-G 2-D 3-B 4-H 5-A 6-E 7-C 8-F

NOTES

NOTES

NOTES

www.ingramcontent.com/pod-product-compliance
Lightning Source LLC
La Vergne TN
LVHW072051080426
835508LV00030B/3459